Life Cycles

A Buttertly's Life Cycle

by Jamie Rice

Bullfrog Books

Ideas for Parents and Teachers

Bullfrog Books let children practice reading informational text at the earliest reading levels. Repetition, familiar words, and photo labels support early readers.

Before Reading

- Discuss the cover photo. What does it tell them?

- Look at the picture glossary together. Read and discuss the words.

Read the Book

- "Walk" through the book and look at the photos. Let the child ask questions. Point out the photo labels.

- Read the book to the child, or have him or her read independently.

After Reading

- Prompt the child to think more. Ask: A butterfly has four life stages. Can you name them?

Bullfrog Books are published by Jump!
5357 Penn Avenue South
Minneapolis, MN 55419
www.jumplibrary.com

Library of Congress Cataloging-in-Publication Data

Names: Rice, Jamie, author.
Title: A butterfly's life cycle / by Jamie Rice.
Description: Bullfrog books. Minneapolis, MN: Jump!, Inc., [2023] | Series: Life cycles Includes index. | Audience: Ages 5–8
Identifiers: LCCN 2021048367 (print)
LCCN 2021048368 (ebook)
ISBN 9781636908229 (hardcover)
ISBN 9781636908236 (paperback)
ISBN 9781636908243 (ebook)
Subjects: LCSH: Butterflies—Life cycles —Juvenile literature.
Classification: LCC QL544.2 .R529 2023 (print) LCC QL544.2 (ebook)
DDC 595.78/9156—dc23/eng/20211004
LC record available at
https://lccn.loc.gov/2021048367
LC ebook record available at
https://lccn.loc.gov/2021048368

Editor: Eliza Leahy
Designer: Emma Bersie

Photo Credits: Kim Howell/Shutterstock, cover; irin-k/Shutterstock, 1; PhotonCatcher/Shutterstock, 3 (left); Ziga Camernik/Shutterstock, 3 (right); davidtclay/Shutterstock, 4, 23tr; aslysun/ Shutterstock, 5; Muhammad Naaim/Shutterstock, 6–7, 22t; Stan Kujawa/Alamy, 8, 23tm, 23bm; Mathisa _ s/iStock, 9, 13, 23tl, 23br; Jay Ondreicka/ Shutterstock, 10–11; James Urbach/SuperStock, 12, 23bl; Amanda Melones/Dreamstime, 14–15; ckio/ Shutterstock, 16–17; Leena Robinson/Shutterstock, 18–19; Ken Donaldson/Shutterstock, 20–21; N.R.A Seno Aji/Shutterstock, 22mr; Young Swee Ming/ Shutterstock, 22b; Lawrence Wee/Shutterstock, 22ml; ColleenSlater Photography/Shutterstock, 24.

Printed in the United States of America at Corporate Graphics in North Mankato, Minnesota.

Table of Contents

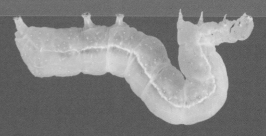

Crawl and Fly

This is a chrysalis.

A butterfly comes out!

How did it get here?

Let's see!

Adult females lay eggs.
The eggs stick to plants.

egg

Days go by.
Caterpillars hatch.

caterpillar · · · ▶

egg
case

They eat the egg cases.
Yum!

They eat plants.

They grow.

They get big.

They crawl.

They molt.
They do this many times!

shed
skin

chrysalis ····▶

Then a caterpillar
grows a chrysalis.

This case keeps it safe.

Weeks go by.
It grows.
Its body changes.

wing

It breaks out!
Now it is a butterfly.
It has wings.

It flies!

It finds food.

It will lay eggs, too.

Life Cycle of a Butterfly

A butterfly's life cycle has four stages. Take a look!

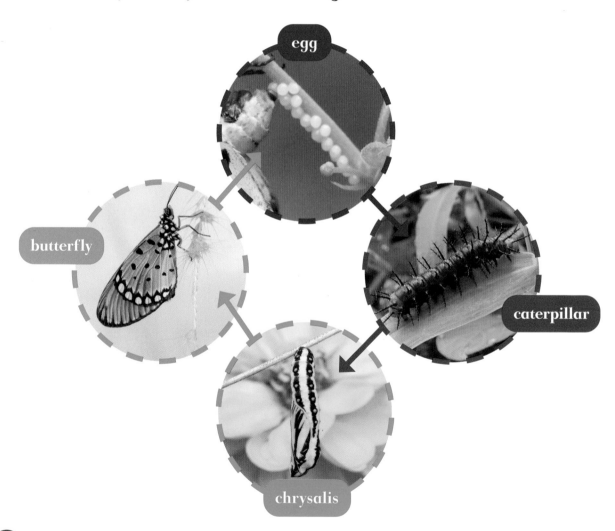

egg

butterfly

caterpillar

chrysalis

Picture Glossary

cases
The outer coverings of objects.

caterpillars
Larvae that change into butterflies or moths.

chrysalis
A butterfly in the stage of growth between caterpillar and adult.

crawl
To move slowly on short legs.

hatch
To break out of eggs.

molt
To shed skin and replace it with new skin.

Index

To Learn More

FACT SURFER

Finding more information is as easy as 1, 2, 3.

❶ Go to www.factsurfer.com

❷ Enter "abutterfly'slifecycle" into the search box.

❸ Choose your book to see a list of websites.